Fine Print

Fine Print

*A Story about
Johann Gutenberg*

by Joann Johansen Burch
illustrations by Kent Alan Aldrich

A Carolrhoda Creative Minds Book

Carolrhoda Books, Inc./Minneapolis

Jacket photo of the Gutenberg Bible reproduced by courtesy of the Library of Congress.

Kent Alan Aldrich created the original artwork for this book by carving his designs by hand into linoleum blocks. The linoleum cutting process is similar to that used for book illustrations in Johann Gutenberg's time when designs were carved into blocks of wood.

Library of Congress Cataloging-in-Publication Data

Burch, Joann Johansen.
    Fine print : a story about Johann Gutenberg / by Joann Johansen Burch ; illustrations by Kent Alan Aldrich.
        p.   cm. — (Creative minds)
    Includes bibliographical references.
    Summary: Recounts the story of the German printer credited with the invention of printing with movable type.
    ISBN 0-87614-682-5 (lib. bdg.)
    1. Gutenberg, Johann, 1397?-1468—Juvenile literature.
2. Printing—History—Origin and antecedents—Juvenile literature.
3. Printers—Germany—Biography—Juvenile literature.
[1. Gutenberg, Johann, 1397?-1468. 2. Printers. 3. Printing—History.]
I. Aldrich, Kent Alan, ill. II. Title. III. Series: Creative minds (Minneapolis, Minn.)
Z126.Z7B87   1991
686.2′092—dc20
[B]   91-11130
                                                            CIP
                                                             AC

Manufactured in the United States of America

1 2 3 4 5 6 7 8 9 10 00 99 98 97 96 95 94 93 92 91

Table of Contents

Author's Note

Writing a book on the life of Johann Gutenberg is not easy, because few facts are available. No one knows exactly when he was born or when he died. Writers and historians must become detectives to gather information on his life.

Histories written after his death tell conflicting stories about how Johann invented printing by machine. Court records from the 1400s can help us figure out how he developed his invention. Johann was involved in a number of lawsuits, and the testimony of witnesses tells his story. Sometimes the testimony can be very dramatic, as when Andreas Dritzehen, one of Johann's partners, argued with his neighbor. At other times, the testimony stops just short of telling us important facts about Johann and his work.

Today the Gutenberg Bible, the first book ever printed in the Western world, is one of the world's treasures. And Johann Gutenberg is remembered as the man who gave us the gift of printed books.

New Terms

adjustable mold: A small wooden box with one side wall that moves to adjust for letters of different widths. A block of metal called a matrix slips in to form the bottom of the box. Hot liquid metal is poured into the top to make a piece of type.

apprentice: Someone who works without pay for a more skilled worker in order to learn a trade.

binder: A person who sews the loose sheets of a book together and binds them between wooden boards covered with cloth, leather, or other materials.

chronicles: Histories or stories that tell of important events in years past and speak of famous people and the great things they have done.

guild: A group of people who make and sell things. Guilds protect their members and make sure they produce high-quality goods.

gulden: A unit of money used in medieval Germany.

illuminator: An artist who decorates books with borders and small paintings.

manuscript: A book written out by hand.

matrix: A model of a letter. A matrix is made by striking a punch into a small bar of metal. The punch leaves the shape of a letter in the metal bar.

medieval: Belonging to the Middle Ages, a period of time from about the year A.D. 500 to the late 1400s.

monastery: A building where monks, priests, and other religious persons live.

movable type: Sticks of metal only a few inches long with a raised letter of the alphabet on one end. Type can be arranged and rearranged in different combinations to form words. The letter on the end of a piece of type is backward. Only when ink is applied and paper is pressed against type, will it "read right," or look like the letters on this page.

parchment: Animal skin from a calf, sheep, or goat that is soaked, stretched, and scraped until smooth enough to write on.

pilgrims: People who travel to an important religious place to ask a special favor of God.

punch: A steel bar with a raised letter carved into one end. Punches are used to make a model of a letter or a matrix. A punch, like a piece of type, reads backward.

rubricator: A person who writes chapter titles and section headings in red in a book to make them stand out from the black letters of the text.

scribe: A person who makes a living from copying books by hand.

vellum: A fine parchment made from the skin of a newly born calf, lamb, or goat.

①

A Long, Cold Winter

During the winter of 1410-1411, twelve-year-old Johann Gutenberg grew restless. He couldn't play outside while snowstorms swirled around his house. He couldn't walk through the forests at the edge of town with snow piled high against the trees. Sometimes he couldn't go to school with his friends, when icy winds froze everything in their path.

Fortunately there were books in his home, and Johann knew how to read. After he read all of his father's books, he borrowed others from his parents' friends. The nearby monastery also had books he could read, although the most precious ones were chained to reading tables.

Not that Johann would have wanted to take the monastery's books home to read. Most books in the 1400s were about religion, philosophy, law, and other similar topics. Six hundred years ago, there were no books written for children. But good stories could be found in books. When Johann's older brother Friele was too busy to play chess or backgammon, and his sister Else was doing needlework, he could find good company in the history books and chronicles in his father's library. Chronicles told of important events in years past and spoke of famous people and the great things they had done. After Johann was much older, chroniclers wrote about the winter of 1410-1411 and the town of Mainz.

Johann, his brother, sister, father, and mother lived in Mainz, where they were born. Nowadays Mainz is a city in Germany. In the 1400s, Mainz was part of the Holy Roman Empire, which included small kingdoms and towns stretching from Germany to northern Italy. Mainz was an important trading town on the Rhine River. Traders came up the river from all parts of Europe and beyond. Johann's parents bought expensive things such as glass from Italy, spices from China, and beautiful books from Germany and beyond.

The books were called manuscripts from a Latin word meaning "written by hand." All books were copied down with pen and ink, letter by letter. Manuscript books sometimes took a long time to make and could be very expensive. Six hundred years ago, a luxury book might be worth as much as a good-sized farm.

Besides buying books from traders, Johann's father paid local copyists, called scribes, to copy texts by hand. When the text was finished, the scribe handed the buyer a set of loose sheets covered with neat handwriting. The loose pages were made of calf-, sheep-, or goatskins called parchment or vellum. The skins had been soaked, stretched, and scraped until they were smooth enough to write on.

Before the sheets of parchment became a book, many more craftspeople did their work. Johann, anxious to read every new book his father ordered, followed each step. The loose sheets first went to the rubricator, or "red inker." The rubricator wrote chapter titles and section headings in red to make them stand out from the black letters of the text. Sometimes the rubricator also put a red line through the first letter of each sentence.

Parchment was so expensive that none of it could be wasted. If any space was left at the bottom of the page, a new chapter started right after the one before. Since every inch of space was used, the rubricator's work helped readers find their place on the page.

Next, Johann's father might give the pages to an artist called an illuminator. Illuminators decorated the margins with miniature scenes, geometric designs, or borders of leaves and flowers. For more expensive books, illuminators painted brightly colored pictures or giant letters at the beginning of each chapter. On the most precious books, thin sheets of gold leaf were applied to make the pages shine.

The final step was a trip to the bindery. The binder sewed the loose sheets of parchment together and bound them between wooden boards. At the bindery, workers also covered the boards with cloth, leather, or perhaps even gold, silver, and carved ivory. For fancier leather covers, the title of the book was stamped on, one letter at a time, with brass punches.

Johann grew impatient waiting for books to be finished. He wished for a faster way to make them. A scribe spent weeks copying a book.

Then, by the time the rubricator, illuminator, and binder did their jobs, several months might pass. There must be a better way, Johann thought, and someday he would figure it out.

In the meantime, he had other things, like school, to think about. Johann's father saw to it that he and his brother received a good education. At that time, boys like Johann went to schools run by the Catholic church. In school priests taught them their most important subject: Latin. During school hours, students and teachers read and spoke only in Latin. It wasn't easy to study grammar, geography, or arithmetic in a foreign language!

At school Johann used the name Gutenberg, even though his brother and the rest of his family were called Gensfleisch. The Gensfleisch family was a large one, and several men in Mainz were named Johann Gensfleisch. Johann may have preferred being called Gutenberg, or "good hill," to Gensfleisch, which means "goose flesh."

Johann took his name from Hof zum Gutenberg, one of the three mansions his family owned. *Hof* in German means "court." Large medieval houses like Hof zum Gutenberg were often U-shaped with an inner courtyard. The rooms around the courtyard had doors and glass windows to let in light and air. On stormy winter days when he couldn't go outside, Johann read beside the windows. They gave better light than the flickering wax candles he lit at night.

Most houses in Mainz did not have glass windows or wax candles for lighting. They were dark and smoky places. In the daytime, some light came in through narrow windows covered with oiled cloth. But at night and during cold weather, wooden shutters closed out any natural light. Since candles were expensive, the glowing fire in the fireplace was often the only source of light. People cooked meals in the fireplace, and smoke drifted around the room. Sometimes it was hard to breathe, and the walls became covered with black soot.

Hof zum Gutenberg did have one thing in common with other houses in Mainz: no indoor plumbing. This meant no bathroom was inside. Johann and his family used an outhouse in the backyard. In colder weather and at night, they used indoor pots which had to be emptied often. There may have been a steam room in the basement of Hof zum Gutenberg for bathing. If not, Johann would have gone to a public or private bathhouse, as everyone else did in Mainz.

On his way to the bathhouse or to school, Johann walked down narrow, twisting streets. Rows of houses lined the streets, and many had shops on the ground floor. The buildings were narrow and tall, sometimes three and four stories high. To gain more living space, each story stuck out a little beyond the one below. Upper floors jutted over the street, and houses opposite each other almost met above Johann's head.

All through the winter of 1410-1411, snow piled up on the high-pitched roofs and then crashed down to the streets below. Even with the snow and cold weather, Johann could smell the garbage tossed into the gutters. Pigs and chickens running loose through Mainz ate some of the litter, but there were always piles waiting to be cleaned up. If he was unlucky, Johann stepped in a pile when he wasn't looking. And on very unlucky days, he might even get a shower from dirty water thrown out of an upstairs window.

Johann passed by many of the shops lining the streets of Mainz. These shops were run by guilds. In the 1400s in Europe, there were craft guilds and merchant guilds. Men and women who made things to sell were members of the craft guilds.

19

These included jewelers' guilds, weavers' guilds, carpenters' guilds, and many others. Many of the more successful townspeople belonged to merchant guilds. They handled the town's trade. Merchant guilds also supplied craft guilds with the raw materials they needed. Jewelers, for example, bought gold through merchant guilds, and weavers bought dyes.

The men in Johann's family were not guild members. They had inherited money and property and did not need to work. However, many of them did work, especially in the town's government. Johann and his family were members of a group of high-ranking families known as patricians. They had lived in Mainz for many years and were very powerful. The patrician families operated the mint, which made the town's money. The mint was also in charge of collecting taxes to run the town's government.

Collecting taxes was not popular. During the winter of 1410–1411, patricians were becoming very unpopular with the guilds of Mainz.

Johann's father was one of the patrician members of the Mainz town council. Guild members could be on the council too, but there were always more than enough patricians to give them control of Mainz. People in the guilds wanted more of their members on the council. They had been angry for a long time about high taxes the council put on beer, wine, and grain.

In early 1411, times were bad for many Mainz citizens. Most people had not earned enough money to keep their families fed and warm during the long, cold winter. That spring, the council voted to raise taxes. Guild members were angrier than ever before. Their families were hungry, and the government wanted even more money from them. The guilds had had enough. They stormed into the town hall, threw out the patricians, and took over the Mainz town council.

Johann's father was horrified. Mainz would be ruined. Guilds had no experience in government. Many members could barely read and write.

The patricians, including Johann's father, lost their jobs at the mint. To make matters worse, they were insulted as they walked down the street. Guild members jeered at Johann too, even though he was only thirteen. By late spring of 1411, Johann's father was fed up with life in Mainz. He moved the family to Eltville, seven and a half miles away, where they owned a home in the country.

Finding a Way

Johann spent three years in Eltville, away from the feuds, noises, and smells of Mainz. Finally in 1414, guilds and patricians made their peace. The Gensfleisch family moved back to Hof zum Gutenberg.

Johann's father could once again collect rents on his town properties. Although he got his old job back at the mint, he did not become a member of the town council again.

Now that Johann was sixteen years old and finished with school, he worked with his father. He had spent time at the mint as a boy and was fascinated by everything that was made there. Besides coining money for Mainz, the mint made government seals and other gold and silver objects such as jewelry and picture frames. Always curious about how things worked, Johann learned all he could from the goldsmiths and jewelers at the Mainz mint.

Goldsmiths belonged to one of the most important craft guilds in town. They served a long apprenticeship. Apprentices lived in the home of a master craftsman. They worked without pay for several years while the master taught them a trade. Since Johann was a patrician, he did not have to begin as an apprentice. Patricians were not part of the guild system.

Besides learning how to make coins, Johann made gold and silver jewelry. An important part of jewelry making is cutting and polishing precious stones. A jeweler cuts gems into facets, giving them many sides, so that light reflects off each one. A well-cut jewel shines brightly. Johann practiced on his family's jewels until they sparkled.

Learning to create objects such as coins and jewelry gave Johann an idea. He remembered how bookbinders used small brass punches to stamp letters onto the leather covers of manuscript books. Maybe he could use that technique to find a faster way to make books. Such an invention would give the world more books, something Johann had been dreaming about ever since he had learned how to read. It could also bring him a lot of money. Johann decided to find a way to make his idea work.

His idea was to make separate metal letters and arrange them into words. By setting up a whole page this way, he could print as many copies of a page as he wanted. Johann began to experiment. First he tried to sand-cast metal letters, the way he sand-cast jewelry.

For his jewelry, Johann made a wax model of the piece, just the way he wanted it to look. Then he filled both halves of a box with fine, damp sand. This was his casting box. Johann laid the wax model on top of the sand in one half of the box. Then he closed the other half around the model. When he opened the box and took out the model, its shape was left in the sand. Closing the box again, Johann poured melted metal down a hole into the empty shape. After the metal cooled, he had a copy of the model.

Sand casting did not work very well with letters. Johann went through all the steps for making jewelry. But when the metal hardened and he lifted the letters from the sand, they were so imperfect he had to rework them with a knife.

Johann was even more disappointed when he lined up the metal letters to form words. He spread ink evenly over the letters, put a scrap of parchment on the inky surface, and pressed hard so the letters would press onto the parchment. But no matter how careful he was, the letters came out crooked on the printed page. Not only that, if one letter was just a hair short, it wouldn't get enough ink and would print lighter than the others. Sometimes even parts of the same letter didn't print evenly. He had to find a better way to make his idea work.

Johann's father died in 1419, when Johann was twenty-one years old. Although he received money every year from rents on the properties his father had owned, he continued to work at the Mainz mint. And he still spent most of his spare time working on printing experiments.

When a papermaking shop opened in Mainz, Johann paid a visit. Six hundred years ago, paper was made by hand out of cloth rags. Papermakers beat rags and water to a pulp in large vats. Then they dipped screen-covered molds into the vats to scoop out the paper pulp. After each dip into the vat, a soggy new sheet of paper was transferred onto a piece of felt. Layers of felt and paper were stacked in piles. Others were squashed tight in a press. Each time the papermaker turned a huge wooden screw, the press forced more water out of the paper.

The paper press may have given Johann an idea: What if he could make a press that would squash a single piece of paper against words made from his metal letters? If he put ink on the letters, the force of the press would print the words right onto the paper. No more pressing parchment against the letters by hand as he had done in his earliest printing experiments. A wooden press would be faster and would print more evenly than he had been able to print before. It just might work.

Before Johann could try out his new idea, another wave of trouble with the guilds broke out. In 1428, the guilds took over the town council by force once again. Many patricians were not allowed to own property in Mainz. Others were told to leave town.

Johann was one of those who had to leave. He was tired of guild revolts anyway and decided to move. He would go to Strasbourg, one hundred miles down the Rhine River from Mainz. With the money his father had left him, he could spend all his time trying to make his printing experiments work.

A Secret Workshop

Johann had heard that people in Strasbourg liked books as much as he did. He knew Strasbourg had a cathedral, with a library full of fine books. A city where others were interested in books and learning would be a good place to work on his printing experiments.

After three days riding his horse through thick forests, Johann reached the walls surrounding the city. Guards at the main gate checked his traveling papers and let him in. He was surprised to see how modern Strasbourg was. The streets were paved with stones. Merchants, clerks, and servant girls walked about. Workmen on high scaffolds were adding a new spire to the cathedral.

Johann settled into a room at an inn and explored Strasbourg. The Gensfleisch family was well known even outside of Mainz, and it was easy for Johann to meet people. But he was not interested in making a lot of friends. He wanted to find a workshop so he could continue his experiments.

When Johann saw the area around the old monastery of St. Arbogast, he knew he had found the perfect place. St. Arbogast was a quiet neighborhood just outside the city walls. Here, Johann would be able to keep his many printing experiments a secret.

Six hundred years ago, trade secrets were closely guarded. Bakers refused to share recipes. Jewelers kept their techniques to themselves. Goldsmiths never revealed to outsiders how they melted and shaped metals. But Johann had learned goldsmithing secrets at the Mainz mint. By using these methods, he thought he could invent a way to produce books not by hand but with metal letters and a press.

Johann set up his workshop in a building in St. Arbogast. He spent long hours working alone, asking for help only when it was absolutely necessary. For his experiments, he needed large quantities of metals. Only a guild member could get them for him, so Johann asked Hanns Dünne, a Strasbourg goldsmith, for help. He paid Hanns one hundred guldens for the metal—enough to buy a house in town or even a farm. Johann was going to make his ideas work, no matter what the cost.

He was still working at his experiments when a messenger came from Mainz three years later. The messenger told Johann that the new government of Mainz would let him return. But Johann didn't want to go back. That would mean moving his workshop, and he had made progress in quiet St. Arbogast.

It wasn't until 1433, five years after his exile, that Johann returned to Mainz. He went back for his mother's funeral, but he didn't stay. With the inheritance from his mother, added to what his father had left him, Johann had enough to buy all the materials he needed...he thought.

Back in Strasbourg, Johann heard some bad news. The Mainz town council said he had to move back if he wanted to keep receiving his share of the family inheritance. The two towns were rivals, and Mainz didn't want its money going to Strasbourg.

Johann was furious. Without the money his parents had left him, he couldn't afford to buy metals, inks, parchment, and paper. But still he wouldn't go back to Mainz. He would rather earn his own money, even if it meant less time for his experiments.

Hanns Dünne said Johann could work in his goldsmithing shop. Word of Johann's skill in cutting and polishing jewels spread throughout the city of Strasbourg. Wealthy people brought their gems for him to shape and polish.

One day Andreas Dritzehen, a Strasbourg patrician, asked Johann to teach him how to cut and polish stones. Johann's first reaction was to say no, because that would take even more time away from inventing. But he finally agreed; he would charge Andreas a fee. If he charged enough, he could pay for his printing supplies.

But Johann always seemed to need more supplies. And supplies cost so much money. In 1434 Johann learned that Nicholas, the Mainz town clerk, was visiting Strasbourg. Still angry about having his inheritance cut off, he had Nicholas arrested.

According to medieval law, this was a legal way to collect money. Mainz owed him 310 guldens, Johann told Nicholas. And Nicholas could stay in jail until Mainz agreed to pay all the money back.

Strasbourg's officials were embarrassed. They wanted to be on friendly terms with Mainz. And here was Johann Gutenberg putting the Mainz town clerk in jail. The officials asked Johann to drop his charges against Nicholas. He refused, saying he wouldn't let Nicholas go until the clerk promised to use his influence to get Johann's money released.

The clerk finally agreed and went back to Mainz. But Johann was given only a small part of what was owed to him. The Mainz town council said he would have to return to get the rest. Johann didn't go back for two reasons: he liked his Strasbourg workshop, and he had fallen in love with a Strasbourg woman.

Her name was Ennelin zu der Iserin Thüre, which means Anne of the Iron Door. She was talented, well traveled, and from a patrician family. Everyone admired her, including Johann. Charmed by her beauty and intelligence, he asked her to marry him. She accepted.

Then Johann changed his mind and decided that he didn't want to get married after all. No one knows why Johann changed his mind. Perhaps at age thirty-eight he felt too set in his ways to marry. Perhaps she wanted him to spend more time with her and less time on his experiments. Whatever reasons he gave, Ennelin was outraged. In 1436 she sued him for breaking his promise to marry her.

Lawsuits were common in the 1400s, and this was the first of many for Johann. The case was heard before the Strasbourg town court. Witnesses who testified for Johann pointed out how well liked and respected he was. Those who had done business with him said he was fair and honest. But Ennelin's shoemaker testified against Johann. This testimony made Johann so angry, he called the shoemaker "a miserable wretch who lives by cheating and lying."

The judge ruled in Johann's favor, so he did not have to pay Ennelin the large sum of money she asked for. But Johann's troubles weren't over. The shoemaker sued Johann for damaging his reputation by calling him a liar and a cheat. In that lawsuit, the judge ruled in the shoemaker's favor. Johann had to pay a heavy fine of fifteen guldens.

Fifteen guldens to a shoemaker! He could have used that money to buy materials for his experiments. This really made Johann angry. However, he soon thought of a way to replace the money.

In 1439 a great fair was to be held in Aachen. Relics of Jesus Christ were put on display every seven years. There were clothes that Jesus was said to have been wrapped in after he was born. The dress his mother Mary was supposed to have worn when she gave birth was also on display. So was the cloth Jesus was thought to have worn at his crucifixion. People came from all over Europe to view the relics. Called pilgrims, they came to ask a special favor of God, perhaps to be cured of an illness, or to be forgiven for sins.

Johann planned to make badges to sell to the pilgrims to show that they had been to Aachen. He asked his friend Hans Riffe, an important man in Strasbourg, to be his partner. Riffe would pay for the materials and receive one-third of the profits. Johann would make the badges and collect the remaining two-thirds of the money.

As soon as Andreas Dritzehen heard about Johann's new business, he asked to become a partner. And when Father Anthony Heilmann heard about it, he asked if his brother Andreas could join also. Father Heilmann offered to pay Johann a fee for teaching his brother.

Here was a way to make even more money from the pilgrim badges. The two Andreases would pay Johann eighty guldens each. Johann drew up an agreement. He would get one half of the profits, Hans Riffe one fourth, and Andreas Dritzehen and Andreas Heilmann would split the other fourth.

They worked hard making badges and hoped to earn a lot of money. The badges were mirrors with metal frames. Mirrors were new in Europe. Johann made them by coating a piece of glass with melted tin or lead. Pilgrims fastened the badges to their hoods or coats to catch a reflection of the relics. It was thought that by catching the reflection of something holy, part of its holiness stayed with the pilgrims forever.

All the time Johann was teaching the others how to make mirrors and polish stones, he continued working on his idea for a faster way to make books. He was making progress in spite of many difficulties, but he was such a perfectionist that he was rarely happy with the results.

Then he learned some terrible news. Dritzehen and Heilmann rushed to Johann's workshop to tell him the Aachen fair had been postponed for a year. Johann was very disappointed. He had counted on profits from the pilgrim badges.

His partners weren't happy either. Now they had to wait a whole year to receive money from their work. When they looked around the St. Arbogast workshop, they asked about the tools and metals lying around. Could Johann be hiding something from them? After all, they said, they were all partners, and he shouldn't keep secrets from them. They asked him to teach them whatever he was doing. Johann promised to think about it.

After they left, Johann debated his future. Should he go back to Mainz, where there was money waiting for him? Or should he stay in Strasbourg, where he thought his invention was close to working? He looked over the metal letters he had made: He called them type. He took stock of the finished type, so carefully arranged in a box in alphabetical order. It was all nearly perfect.

Johann was proud of his work so far, and when everything was perfect he would have a remarkable invention. He didn't want to leave St. Arbogast when he was this close to success. So he decided to let his partners in on part of his secret in exchange for money—a lot of it. But he would not tell them everything.

Johann Shares His Secret

Johann told Dritzehen and Heilmann about his plans. He was going to invent a way to make more copies of one manuscript in just a few days than all the scribes in Mainz—or in all of Europe—could make during *the rest of their lives*. When he did, he would earn a fortune. Anyone who invested money in his project would earn a fortune also.

Right now, he told them, he needed money for materials. He thought he needed a year or two to work out a few minor problems. Once these were solved, books could be made by metal letters and a press, rather than by hand.

His partners were eager to learn about the invention and share in the fortune to be made.

Dritzehen and Heilmann agreed to invest 250 guldens more, for a total of 410 guldens. Johann asked them to pay fifty guldens in cash and the rest in payments over the next few years. He also made them promise to keep everything a secret. Johann drew up an agreement. It stated that if any partner should die before the contract ended in 1443, no new partners could join.

Unlike Heilmann, whose brother paid the fifty guldens for him, Dritzehen could only come up with forty. To get that much he had taken out a loan on the property he inherited from his father. And he asked the farmer renting his land to sell off some of the grain. But that brought in only a small amount.

Dritzehen was such a good craftsman that Johann was willing to wait for the remaining ten guldens. Dritzehen was sure Johann's invention would be making money before the next payment was due, and he would no longer be in debt.

Johann showed his partners the basic goldsmithing techniques of melting metals. The partners would not be sand-casting letters as Johann had done before. They would be using three tools that Johann had perfected over the years: the punch, the matrix, and the mold.

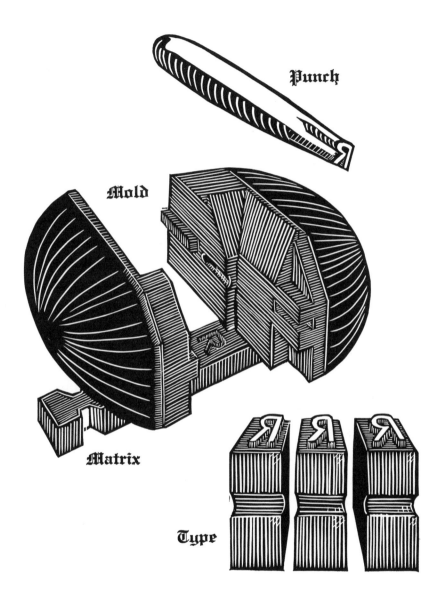

Punch

Mold

Matrix

Type

41

To make a punch, he cut a letter into the narrow, pointed end of a steel bar. He scraped and filed the letter again and again until it was perfectly shaped. Johann's punches were similar to those used by bookbinders. Except when Johann wanted to check his design, he didn't pound the punch into a leather book cover. Instead, he held the punch over a flame until it was covered with soot. Then he pressed the sooty punch against a piece of paper and looked at the printed letter for any flaws.

For the matrix, he heated a bar of copper or brass. Here his skill in working with metal came in handy. With a hammer, Johann carefully pounded the punch into the bar. When he removed the punch, the shape of the letter remained stamped into the bar. This bar became a model, or matrix, of the letter.

Then Johann stuck the matrix into the bottom of a small wooden frame. This was his mold. He poured hot liquid metal into the mold. He jerked hard, so the metal filled all corners of the mold and matrix. When the metal cooled and hardened, Johann removed it from the mold. The hardened metal, called a piece of type, was a stick only a few inches long. On one end was a raised letter.

Johann's idea was to stand the metal sticks, letter end facing up, in a press. He would make words, sentences, paragraphs, whole pages of little metal letters. But first he needed to make more type.

Dritzehen and Heilmann used punch, matrix, and mold to make type for all the letters of the alphabet. Johann showed them how to adjust the mold for skinny letters like *i* and *l* and for fat ones like *m* and *w*. He had discovered earlier that when he didn't adjust for width, the letters would print l i ke t h i s.

Dritzehen and Heilmann made many pieces of type, since Johann used the same letter a number of times when he set up a page. He was still having problems keeping the type from slipping and printing crookedly. He needed to find a way to line up the letters and keep them even while he printed them.

Johann asked Conrad Sahspach, a special kind of carpenter called a joiner, to make a better frame to hold the type in place. He also asked him to make a printing press. The most important part of the press was a large wooden screw attached to a long handle. Only a joiner would have the skill to carve such a screw.

The press was set up at Dritzehen's house in

town. No outsider could see the entire printing process in one place. That way the secret would be safe. Dritzehen spent his days at St. Arbogast with Johann. At night, he carried on experiments in his home, trying out type on the press.

Barbara de Zabern, his neighbor, often saw Dritzehen working late at night. One time she came over. "Don't you want to go to bed at all today?" she asked.

"I must do this first." Dritzehen continued busily arranging the press.

Barbara asked him what he was doing. He told her he was making mirrors for the Aachen fair. That was the answer the partners had decided to give anyone who became curious about their secret work.

Barbara continued to talk to Dritzehen. "But goodness, what a sum of money you seem to be spending. Why, all those things must have cost at least ten guldens."

Dritzehen, worn out with working so much, shouted, "You are a simpleton.... Listen, if you had all it has cost me over three hundred guldens, you would have enough to last you all your life. I have sunk both my cash and my inheritance into the matter."

"But if it should turn out badly, what would you do then?" she asked.

"It can't turn out badly," he replied. "Before a year is over, we shall have back again all our money, and be well off forever."

Overwork ruined Dritzehen's health. Shortly before Christmas, he became ill. Johann sent his servant to Dritzehen's house to bring back the type. In December of 1438, Andreas Dritzehen died, penniless.

After Dritzehen's death, Johann did something that is hard to believe. He melted down all the metal type they had spent so much time making. Since the type had been in Dritzehen's house, his relatives might claim it as a part of their inheritance. Johann didn't want to risk that. He would rather start over again than have anyone else learn his secret.

When Heilmann heard about Dritzehen's death, he ran to Conrad Sahspach's house. "Conrad," he said, "since Dritzehen is dead, and as you made the presses and are in on the secret, go and take the press at Dritzehen's to pieces so that no one can tell what it is." When Sahspach arrived, the press was already in pieces. Johann probably got there first.

Andreas Dritzehen's older brother, George, demanded that he and his brother Nicholas take Andreas's place in the partnership. George was a minor Strasbourg official known for his bad temper. When Johann told him there could be no new partners, George decided to take Johann to court. George wanted all the money Andreas had invested. Johann's contract with his partners protected him from these kinds of claims. The contract set a very low limit on what Andreas's heirs could expect to receive. But Andreas had been absent-minded. Although he had the contract with him when he died, he had never bothered to sign it.

In 1439 Johann found himself in court again. He worried that the secret of his printing experiments would come out during the trial. But his partners refused to talk about their work. Johann pleaded with the judge to rule against George and Nicholas Dritzehen.

The lawsuit lasted a year. Johann's experiments were at a standstill until the court finally ruled in his favor. After the trial, he went back to his workshop. But most of the partnership money had been spent, and Johann's remaining partners wouldn't contribute any more guldens. Johann took a loan from a Strasbourg church, but after that money was gone, no one else would lend him any more.

He seemed further from making a success of his ideas than when he first talked to his partners about making books from metal letters. Johann Gutenberg decided to go back to Mainz and collect his inheritance.

Making It Work

Johann returned to his hometown, collected his inheritance, and set up a printing shop. He was eager to make his invention work.

In Strasbourg he had made type from lead, but lead type wore out quickly, the way the tip of a pencil wears down. Now Johann tried mixing other metals with lead. Metal cost a lot of money, and Johann spent all of his inheritance buying different kinds. In 1448 he took out yet another loan.

He mixed tin with lead, but the letters were still too soft. Harder metals such as iron and zinc took too long to melt. Others shrank when they cooled. Finally, Johann found the right combination: lead and antimony.

In 1450, after working on his experiments for nearly thirty years, Johann was ready to begin printing. He knew just what he wanted to print: the Bible, the most important book he could imagine. But now he had no money for such a large project. Johann looked around Mainz for someone to invest in his invention.

James Fust, a goldsmith he knew, had a brother, also named Johann. Johann Fust was a wealthy businessman and lawyer. Fust hadn't inherited money as Gutenberg had, but he had done well in business. Johann convinced Fust to put money into his invention. He talked of a machine and metal letters that could make a hundred, or even a thousand, copies of the same page, all exactly the same.

Fust asked Johann if a loan of eight hundred guldens would be enough to build presses and make type to print the Bible. With that amount, Johann said he would be ready to make two hundred copies of the most beautiful Bible ever seen.

The printing would be more perfect than even the best scribe could create.

Eight hundred guldens was a lot of money, enough to buy a hundred fat oxen or several large farms. Fust was a careful man and drove a hard bargain. He made Johann sign an agreement. If Johann didn't repay the loan, plus interest, in five years, then Fust would get all the printing presses, tools, and materials. These were harsh terms, but Johann was willing to do anything to give his invention a chance to work.

It took Johann two years to set up a workshop and make all the preparations for printing the Bible. He hired an assistant, Peter Schöffer. Schöffer had spent years as a scribe copying manuscripts by hand. Like Johann, he was a perfectionist. Under Johann's teaching, Schöffer became an expert at making type. He helped design a smaller size of type when Fust wanted to fit more words onto each page. Fust, always careful with his money, figured it would cost one-third less to print the Bible with smaller type.

Schöffer trained the shop's workers to make metal type. Johann had several presses built and showed the workers how to set up pages of type in the flat bed of the press.

He also taught them how to grind and mix ink. This was another part of the invention. Johann's ink had to be wet enough to evenly coat the leather-covered balls used to ink the type. And it had to be thick enough to stick to the type without running. Johann's ink was made from linseed oil and lampblack, a fine soot.

By the end of 1452, Johann was fifty-four years old, and he was ready to begin printing. The moment he had worked toward for more than thirty years had finally arrived. He was proud of his work and ready to show his invention to the world. However, he had already spent all the eight hundred guldens from Fust's loan. Before he could print, he needed more money.

Fust offered him eight hundred guldens more, only if he became Johann's partner. Johann did not want Fust as his partner. The invention of movable type was Johann's idea, and he didn't care to share it with anyone. But there was no other way to get the money he needed. Taking on an unwanted partner would be temporary, Johann reasoned. As soon as he made a profit on the Bibles, he would get out of the partnership.

Why did Johann need so much money? Printing the Bible was a huge project. In addition to paying his workers, Johann paid a joiner to make several presses. He bought metal for type and enough vellum and paper to print about 180 copies of the Bible. About thirty copies would be printed on vellum, and the rest on paper, which was cheaper.

Adding up Johann's paper bill shows how some of Fust's money was spent. Five hundred sheets of good writing paper cost one gulden. Three hundred and twenty-one sheets of paper were used in each Bible. For that many sheets of vellum, Johann had to buy nearly half as many skins. Altogether Johann used more than five thousand skins!

Two years went by and still the Bible wasn't finished. Johann was always trying to improve his invention. If even one letter was blurred, he threw away the whole page and made a new piece of type. Each printed page had to be clear and sharp, or it wouldn't go into his Bible.

Johann was also spending time making two new sets of type for a book of Psalms that Fust wanted to print next. In addition Johann may have had a printing shop of his own that Fust didn't know about. Doing small printing jobs on the side may have helped Johann earn his living during the years he spent working on the Bible.

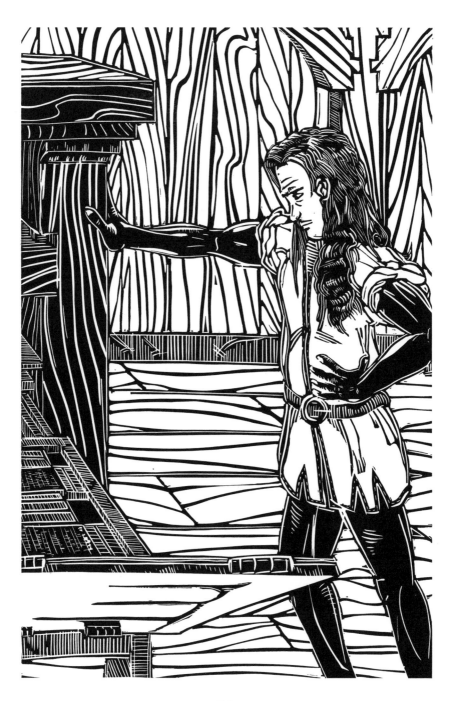

Five years after Fust made the first loan to Johann, he sued to get all his money back, plus interest, a full 2,026 guldens. No one knows why Fust did this only months before the Bible was completed. Perhaps he found out about the other printing shop and thought Johann was cheating him. Or perhaps Fust realized Johann was going to end the partnership once the Bible was printed. The way Fust saw it, either he or Johann would win money and fame for making the first printed book. By suing Johann, Fust made sure he would be the winner.

On November 6, 1455, in the dining hall of the Convent of the Barefoot Friars, Fust's lawsuit was heard. The judge ruled in favor of Fust. Johann would have to pay Fust the original loan, plus interest, and whatever part of the second loan that Johann had spent on his own printing shop.

Betrayed

The lawsuit was a complete surprise to Johann. He didn't have the money to pay Fust back, so he had to turn over his tools, printing presses, and the almost-completed Bibles. Fust then asked Peter Schöffer, who was engaged to his daughter, to be his partner. For many years, people gave the new printing company of Fust and Schöffer all the credit for producing the Bible, the world's first printed book.

History has been kinder to Johann. The first printed book is now called the Gutenberg, or 42-line, Bible. The Bible was printed from the smaller type Fust asked Johann to make to save space. On each page, there are two columns, each with forty-two lines of text, hence the name 42-line Bible.

In 1455 or 1456, when the Bible was completed, few people realized how important Johann's invention would become. How could Johann himself have guessed that printing from movable type would change the world? At the time, Johann felt betrayed. Not only had he lost control of his invention, he had also lost all hope of making a fortune from it. But Johann did not give up, for he knew more about printing than anyone else in the world.

He set up shop in his home and continued to print small books, pamphlets, and calendars. He may have moved away from Mainz for a time. In 1459 another edition of the Bible came on the market in Bamberg, some distance away on the Main River. It was printed from large type and is called the 36-line Bible, because each page has two columns of thirty-six lines each. Although Johann never put his name on anything he printed, some historians believe he was responsible for this Bible.

It is possible that Johann printed one last book in 1460, the *Catholican*, a huge Latin dictionary and encyclopedia. At the end of the text, the anonymous printer boasts that the book was made "without help of reed, stylus or pen, by the wondrous agreement, proportion, and harmony of punches and type."

Slowly, word of Johann's invention spread throughout Europe. Not everyone who saw printed books was as pleased as Johann. One famous book collector, the Italian duke of Urbino, refused to put any printed books in his collection. He preferred the handmade look and feel of manuscript books. Many scribes, too, disliked printed books. Although rubricators, decorators, and binders were still needed to add the finishing touches to printed books, scribes saw their jobs being taken away from them.

Others were more enthusiastic about the new books made from movable type. Cities all over Europe wanted printed books, and young men were sent to Mainz to learn the art of printing. By 1470 Johann's invention had spread to fourteen cities in Europe. Between 1470 and 1480 more than one hundred cities set up printing presses. By the end of the 1400s, printed books could be found throughout western Europe. More than nine million books had been printed before the year 1500. People who might never have been able to buy a manuscript book *could* afford to buy printed books.

Johann Gutenberg's invention changed the world. Printing became a cheap and fast way to spread ideas and knowledge. And it brought ideas and the joy of reading to more people than Johann could have dreamed possible.

How did Johann react to his success? At first he didn't feel very successful at all. When enemy troops attacked Mainz in 1462, Hof zum Gutenberg was burned. Fust's printing shop, and many other businesses, were also set on fire. Quite a few people left town, including many printers, who set up shops in other towns and countries. Printing would never again be such an important business in Johann's hometown.

Nothing is known about Johann during this period until January 17, 1465, when Archbishop Adolph of Mainz appointed him to his personal staff. This didn't mean that Johann had to work for the archbishop. The appointment was an honor.

With it, Johann received a pension for the rest of his life.

The archbishop's certificate of appointment read, in part:

> On account of the conspicuous, welcome, and willing service rendered to Us... by our beloved and loyal Johann Gutenberg... by special favor, we... accept and take him... as our servant and court attendant. Each and every year... we shall have given to him the costume of our gentlemen... and... twenty molders of corn and two fuders of wine... so long as he lives.

At last Johann was treated with respect. The archbishop was proud of the precious gift Johann Gutenberg had given to the town of Mainz. Johann lived the last three years of his life in comfort and security. He died when he was around seventy years old. The date of his death, like everything else about him, is not known exactly, but is usually given as February 3, 1468.

Soon others followed Archbishop Adolph's example and honored Johann. After Johann's death, Peter Schöffer admitted that, after all, Johann

Gutenberg had invented printing. Chroniclers praised Johann's invention. In 1470, a Frenchman summed up the praise in a letter to a friend:

For they say that not far from the city of Mainz, there was a certain Johann who bore the surname Gutenberg, who first of all men thought out the art of printing by which books are made, not written with a reed as former books were made, nor by pen...but by metal letters—and that indeed with speed, elegance and beauty....
Moreover the illustrious Gutenberg invented... letters of such a sort that whatever can be said, or thought, can immediately be written and copied and handed down to the memory of generations that are to come....

Sources

Chappel, Warren. *A Short History of the Printed Word.* New York: Knopf, 1970.

Furhmann, Otto W. *Gutenberg and the Strasbourg Documents of 1439.* New York: Press of the Woolly Whale, 1940.

Ing, Janet. *Johann Gutenberg and His Bible.* New York: The Typophiles, 1988.

McMurtrie, Douglas C. *The Gutenberg Documents.* New York: Oxford University Press, 1941.

Scholderer, Victor. *Johann Gutenberg: The Inventor of Printing.* London: The Trustees of the British Museum, 1963.

For Further Reading

Epstein, Sam and Beryl. *The First Book of Printing.* New York: Franklin Watts, 1975.

Harris, Brayton. *Johann Gutenberg and the Invention of Printing.* New York: Franklin Watts, 1972.

McMurtrie, Douglas C. *Wings for Words.* New York: Rand McNally, 1940.

Ryder, John. *Printing.* London: The Bodley Head, 1960.